PEAK DISTRICT VILLAGES

THE SKETCHES OF BRIAN EDWARDS

VIEW OVER ASHFORD FROM CASTLEGATE   BRIAN EDWARDS 1996.

Volume I: Ashford, Longstone, Hassop, Sheldon, Wardlow, Rowland, Monsal

Introduction

This is the first volume in a series on Peak District Villages. It seems natural that I should start with those villages surrounding my home in Great Longstone and grouped loosely around the Wye Valley. This is an area known for it's white limestone walls and the steep sided Monsal Dale situated between Bakewell and Buxton.

I have lived in the Peak District since 1983 and, prior to that, in Totley some few hundred metres from the National Park. Over these years I have derived so much pleasure from running, walking and cycling through the attractive countryside, often visiting villages during years of fell racing, playing football in local leagues and, latterly, lecturing on sketching and other subjects to local organisations.

There have been many occasions when I have taken my camera and sketchbook to record the villages, trees, surrounding countryside, stiles, bridges and so on. The Peak District isn't all gift shops and historic monuments. It has many small villages and a few market towns where the communities go about their normal life, often working locally and organising their own social activities.Summers in the Peak are often short but compensated by colourful autumns. Winters are harsh, when it snows it snows and the winds can be bitingly cold. We all love the spring - a welcome renewal, wild flowers, tumbling lapwings, lonely curlews and twittering larks.

It is heart-warming to see that despite continual problems for farmers in recent years, many villages have working farms and the scurrying back and forth of tractors whether laden with hay or manure is thankfully a common sight. Who, but the impatient, objects to being held up by a flock of sheep being driven to new pastures or the daily procession of cows plodding slowly along. There's an opportunity to chat to the cheery herdsman and perhaps ask those searching questions about the hard life of these peak farms. The area is one principally of green and white; the limestone taken from the hills to build the many thousands of stone walls and then used in local architecture. The pattern of green fields is confused on days when clouds sweep swiftly over blue skies casting never-to-be-repeated shadows across the land. And who has not been delighted by the strong sunset silhouetting those skeletal clumps of trees which often give away the upturned ground of long disused lead mines.

Amidst all these wonders sit the small villages covered in this book and which make my trips between them on the many footpaths and lanes a journey of discovery. Sadly I do not have space in this volume to feature all the buildings and views in this area. I sincerely hope you enjoy looking at the illustrations which may either remind you of or introduce you to this marvellous area of the Peak District.

Brian Edwards

Great Longstone 1998

THE SHEEPDIP ASHFORD   BRIAN EDWARDS 1996

ACKNOWLEDGEMENTS

Michael Stewart of Little Longstone and Sheila Hurst of Great Longstone for help with captions. My wife, Pam, for her support, helpful comments and word processing.

The following for permission to reproduce work in their possession: Bill and Brenda Bentall, Mick and Caroline Briggs, Mr and Mrs A.J.Byrne, Roger Cox, John and Sue Hawkins, Chris & Sue Woods, Peter and Anne Wrench, Geoffrey and Brenda Smith.

Contents

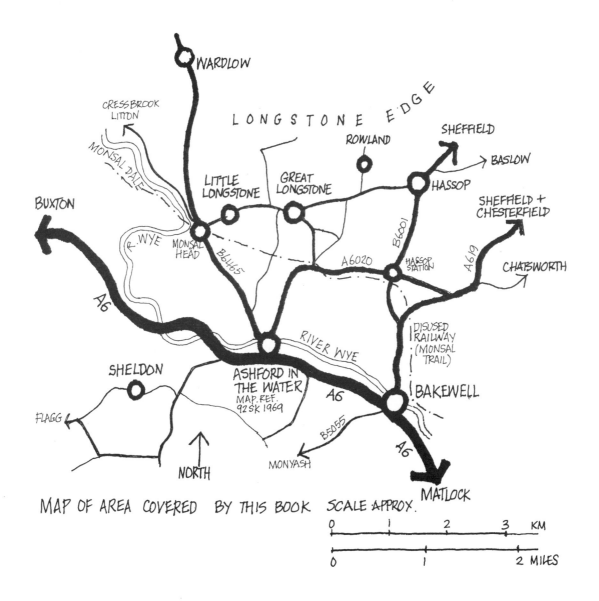

MAP OF AREA COVERED BY THIS BOOK. SCALE APPROX.

WARDLOW

CRESSBROOK
LITTON

LONGSTONE EDGE

ROWLAND

SHEFFIELD

BASLOW

MONSAL DALE

LITTLE
LONGSTONE

GREAT
LONGSTONE

HASSOP

BUXTON

R. WYE

MONSAL
HEAD

B6465

A6020

B6001

HASSOP
STATION

A619

SHEFFIELD +
CHESTERFIELD

CHATSWORTH

A6

RIVER WYE

DISUSED
RAILWAY
(MONSAL
TRAIL)

SHELDON

ASHFORD IN
THE WATER
MAP. REF.
92 SK 1969

A6

BAKEWELL

FLAGG

B5055

A6

NORTH

MONYASH

A6

MATLOCK

0   1   2   3   KM

0   1   2 MILES

Ashford in The Water

Ashford is an attractive village standing to one side of the A6 road 1½ miles north of Bakewell. It's Domesday name, Aisseford, meant 'ford of the ash'. The majority of the older buildings are mainly 18th century.

The village has had a variety of industries, leadmining, buttons, candle and stocking making, sheep farming and the quarrying of black Ashford 'marble' used extensively in church decoration. The dark veins can be seen in many of the limestone walls of the area.

The famous Sheepwash Bridge is possibly one of the most painted and photographed views in Britain and, until recently, sheep were driven across the river for their periodic washing. The stone holding pen is still to be seen on the road side of the River Wye.

The Sheepwash Bridge is a limestone medieval pack horse bridge over the Wye and replaced the original ford on a major ancient route. Beyond can be seen the village and church.

SHEEPWASH BRIDGE 1996 BRIAN EDWARDS
ASHFORD IN THE WATER.

ASHFORD IN THE WATER   BRIAN EDWARDS 1996   THE PUMP.   652

The pump shelter and the church of Holy
Trinity'. Nowadays the water pump has
vanished and only the shelter remains; it is
however the site of one of the well dressings.
Behind the pump is an old 17th century tithe
barn.

page 8

ACROSS FROM THE CHURCH ASHFORD BRIAN EDWARDS 1996.

Although the church was mainly rebuilt in 1870, there are traces of Norman and later work. An excellent and descriptive booklet is on sale in the building.

Cottages on Fennel Street. The herb still
grows abundantly in nooks and crannies
along the road.

The Old School. Ashford in the Water. Brian Edwards 1994.

The 17th century school at Ashford was sadly closed in the 1980's due to diminishing numbers of children in the village. There is an unfortunate flat roofed modern addition (which I have managed to leave out of the drawing) however this is compensated for by the attached schoolmaster's house. The small green in front is the site of one of the well dressings.

BUXTON ROAD ASHFORD IN THE WATER   BRIAN EDWARDS 1996

A number of lanes radiate from the village, above: the old Buxton Road and below: Back Hill Cross which leads out towards Monsal Head.

BACK CROSS ASHFORD-IN-THE-WATER   BRIAN EDWARDS 1996

THE ASHFORD HOTEL ASHFORD-IN-THE-WATER BRIANEDWARDS 3/97.

The Ashford, formerly the Devonshire Arms, stands close by a number of older 18th century cottages and across the road from the village shop.

THE VILLAGE SHOP ASHFORD IN THE WATER

DERBYGATE COTTAGE, ASHFORD-IN-THE-WATER BRIANEDWARDS 1996

Our previous house, Derbygate Cottage, stands on the A6 looking out over the river meadows. Formerly a pair of estate workers cottages for Ashford Hall, it has a fresh water spring in the garden.

ASHFORD HALL DERBYSHIRE
BRIAN EDWARDS MAY 1992

Ashford Hall designed by Joseph Pickard is a mid 18th century house once owned by the Duke of Devonshire when it was occupied by his son, the Marquis of Hartington.

ASHFORD MILL   BRIAN EDWARDS 1986.

The 18th Century Ashford or Flewitts Corn Mill used to have two water wheels serviced by goits passing either side of the mill. The pond, weir and shuttles are still to be seen and occasionally, if you're sharp, a kingfisher or two.

Ashford Derbyshire April 1992
Brian Edwards (Old Lumco Bridge)

Ashford in the Water
Brian Edwards 1990
BE/190

Near the mill is another early packhorse bridge inscribed *M Hyde 1664* which is said to refer to an unfortunate horseman who was thrown over the parapet and drowned in the pool below. Until recent years this bridge carried the main road but these days it is a secluded trout- watching refuge.

One of the six wells dressed each year with tableaux of flower petals pressed into clay.

ASHFORD IN THE WATER, GATE BY THE RIVER.   BRYAN EDWARDS

Downstream several houses enjoy riverside frontages close to one of the several public access points on Watts Green.

In the distance the new road bridge crosses meadows where sheep graze alongside one of the weirs.

The New Bridge Ashford Brian Edwards 6/1997.

As it flows through the village,
the Wye is diverted into a head goit
which feeds water into the Corn Mill.
The most recent bridge shown here
carries the main road away from the old
route to Bakewell.

River and Goit Ashford in the Water Brian Edwards 1996

The yard in front of the old Bulls Head
occasionally hosts folk dancing sessions.

BRIAN EDWARDS 7/1997. THE GRANGE, ASHFORD

One of the pleasant houses on Castle Gate
looks down over meadows to the village.

page 20

This pencil sketch across the old graveyard
captures the modest scale of the older
cottages in the centre of Ashford and shows
the steeply rising ground towards Sheldon.

STILE ON SHADY LANE ASHFORD 1996. BRIAN EDWARDS

ASHFORD, DERBYSHIRE
BRIAN EDWARDS API

This set of stoops is one of several on the way up from Ashford to Little Longstone and crosses Shady lane at this point.

A modest bridge crosses a field brook on Hall End on the edge of the village.

The Rookery is one of the larger houses in Ashford and is approached via a private drive over an old stone bridge spanning the River Wye. Below is a less imposing but no less attractive cottage near Churchdale.

COWS IN THE WYE
ASHFORD 1997/6
BRIAN EDWARDS.

BULLOCK AT ASHFORD
BRIAN EDWARDS 1986.

Upstream from Ashford the Wye winds through meadows much loved by anglers. In this idyllic spot where the air is full of various kinds of insects the cows come down for a drink under the trees. Below the village a young bullock becomes a little too curious for comfort.

GARDEN GATES
THORNBRIDGE   BRIAN EDWARDS 1996

STATUE THORNBRIDGE HALL 1996 BRIAN EDWARDS

THORNBRIDGE HALL STABLES.
1992 BRIANEDWARDS

Sketches around Thornbridge Hall show the fine quality of the stonework. Some of the sculptures were brought from older houses including Chatsworth.

THORNBRIDGE HALL BRIAN EDWARDS 1995

Thornbridge Hall on the road between Longstone and Ashford is a large neo-Tudor house built in the mid 19th century and has a number of interesting lodges and other buildings from the same period. Years of part neglect when owned by Sheffield City Council are currently being redressed by the new owner who is converting this conference centre back to a private dwelling. A public footpath skirts the gardens and affords good views of the hall.

Perfectly sited, close to the main road and alongside the River Wye, stands the charming Riverside Hotel with it's circular dovecote.

THE RIVERSIDE HOTEL ASHFORD BRIAN EDWARDS 6/1997

Sheldon

Sheldon standing at 1000 feet, high above
the Wye Valley, is a typical one-street
settlement lined with limestone cottages and
farms mostly from the 18th century. Once
reliant on lead mining, Sheldon had an influx
of Cornish miners in the 1850's. At one time
the water supply was pumped uphill from
the river about a mile away.

SHELDON CHURCH
BRIAN EDWARDS 1986

An early church built in the middle of the road was demolished in the mid-nineteenth century and a new one, St Michael and All Angels, was erected on the outskirts in 1865.

MAGPIE MINE WINTER
BRIAN EDWARDS 1997.

837

The Magpie Mine at Sheldon is a fine monument to the new ceased lead mining industry which brought prosperity to the Peak District. Constant flooding led to the closure as late as 1958 and nowadays the site is looked after by the Peak District Mines Historical Society.

Dirtlow farm is adjacent to a footpath from Bakewell to Sheldon and is another with commanding views over the Wye Valley. The path passes by a long disused lead rake whose position is marked by a parallel line of trees.

DIRTLOW FARM NEAR SHELDON   BRIAN EDWARDS 1996.

Sheldon sometimes has considerable snow when neighbouring Ashford has none.

This view looks down the only street as it falls steeply towards Ashford a mile or so away.

THE COCK AND PULLET SHELDON 1997 BRIAN EDWARDS.

At one time Sheldon had a pub run by two
old sisters who kept a stern eye on their
customers, occasionally refusing to pour
from their jug if they thought the customer
had drunk enough. That Inn closed some
time ago but in 1996 villagers welcomed the
Cock and Pullet being transformed from an
old building.

TOP COTTAGE AT SHELDON OCTOBER 1995
BRIAN EDWARDS

LOOKING UP THROUGH SHELDON   BRIAN EDWARDS 1996

I always feel that Sheldon appears to be one of the relatively untouched villages in the Peak although obviously a number of cottages and farms have been altered and extended.

Two views on the main street of Sheldon.

page 33

Monsal

MONSAL DALE DEC 85

Monsal Head, a satellite cluster of buildings in the village of Little Longstone, is famous for the dramatic views over the Wye Valley. To the rear rises Fin Cop with it's Stone Age fort remains and in the foreground is the imposing five arched viaduct which once carried the railway line until it's closure in 1959.

Nearby is the now closed 533 yard Headstone tunnel which may be reopened in the future if the plans to re-establish the Matlock - Buxton stretch of railway are realised.

Not far from Monsal Head, one of the finest barns in the area has a series of arches and a sheltered yard. It is good to see that the barn is still well used. From the top of Longstone Moor the view extends over towards the Hope Valley and the moors of the Dark Peak where sparkling white limestone walls give way to dour gritstone.

VIEW FROM LONGSTONE EDGE   BRIAN EDWARDS 1995

There are only a few houses at Monsal Head, a hotel formerly known (along with several others in the district) as the Bulls Head, Monsal Head Cafe and a Stable Bar and gift shop.

This is my final port of call on my periodic journey through the many dales, ghostly quiet in the winter and awash with wild flowers and walkers from spring onwards

UPPERDALE FARM MONSAL BRIAN EDWARDS 1997

STEEL BRIDGE IN MONSAL DALE BRIAN EDWARDS '97

Down below in the valley are just a few old farms and cottages sitting peacefully by the placid trout filled Wye. Many paths follow and cross the various dales such as Monsal, Millers, Chee, Ravens and Monks and after years of walking here I still find new routes.

Wardlow

WARDLOW CHURCH   BRIAN EDWARDS 1997.

The Church and Village Hall

Wardlow is another small one-street upland village lined with farm buildings and once relied on lead mining and sheepfarming. It achieved notoriety for having the last gruesome gibbet occupant in 1815. Nowadays we admire the old field systems and nearby the spectacular view over Ravensdale on our circular route from Longstone to Litton and back.

WARDLOW FARM BRIAN EDWARDS 1996

One of the farms along the Main Street in Wardlow is typical of the area.

FARM WARDLOW BRIAN EDWARDS 1996

WARDLOW STREET 1996 BRIAN EDWARDS

Wardlow has two pubs - The Bulls Head shown here - and The Three Stags Heads on the outskirts at Wardlow Mires. The former can be traced back to 1723 and no doubt profited in the days when there were 27 lead mines around the village.

WARDLOW

Please drive carefully

Wardlow at Christmas 1995
Brian Edwards.

Wardlow is set up high near the Chesterfield
to Chapel-en-le-Frith road. The nearby hills
are criss-crossed with limestone walls
towards Castleton and the Dark Peak.

Little Longstone

LITTLE LONGSTONE
BRIAN EDWARDS 1995

Little Longstone is hidden away in a hollow
between Great Longstone and Monsal Head.
I am sure that is why the flowers in front of
the cottages are so abundant catching all-day
sun and sheltered from the strong winds.
The village is fortunate in still having the
pinfold, (for stray animals) stocks and pump.

WALK TO LITTLE LONGSTONE   BRIAN EDWARDS 1996

SHEEP AT LITTLE LONGSTONE   BRIAN EDWARDS 1996

The footpath approaches to Little Longstone cross fields full of quietly grazing sheep who stamp their feet with surprising strength if you go too near their lambs.

No trip to Little Longstone is complete
without a peep at the old Packhorse Inn
whose name hints at the age and purpose of
the village street.

BRIAN EDWARDS 1996.
BY LITTLE LONGSTONE HALL.

The way out of Little Longstone passes a recently restored line of stone troughs and then presents you with a choice of routes along lane or paths towards it's larger neighbour, Great Longstone.

This area abounds with footpaths between the villages. Above: the path from Great Longstone to Wardlow rounds the side of Longstone Edge.

A heavily rusticated Little Longstone Congregational Church opened in 1844 and despite a distant two year closure recently celebrated it's 150th anniversary.

Christmas Cottage, one of a number in the row lining the narrow street in Little Longstone.

Just up the lane is the Outrake, once a private school and now converted into a number of dwellings.

CHRISTMAS COTTAGE AT LITTLE LONGSTONE BRIAN EDWARDS 7/1997.

'APPROACHING LITTLE LONGSTONE
FROM MONSAL HEAD BRIAN EDWARDS '98

COTTAGES AT LITTLE LONGSTONE BRIAN EDWARDS 1996.

Old cottages at Little Longstone. Nearby the
stone posts of the old village stocks are still
visible together with a fine 16th century
house.

STILES AND GATES LITTLE LONGSTONE 1996 BRIAN EDWARDS.

One approach across the fields from the Monsal Trail brings you to Little Longstone Manor, home of the Longsdon family for many generations. The 18th century house of limestone and gritstone has an impressive range of outbuildings - watch out for the white doves.

Nowadays some of the redundant farm
buildings have been converted into camping
barns and holiday homes. However
Longstone Byre has made a fine family
dwelling with views over Wye valley.
Longstone Edge can be made out rising
behind the house.

BRIAN EDWARDS 1022   VILLAGE GREEN GREAT LONGSTONE 3/98

Great Longstone is a delightful village deriving it's name from 'Langes Dune 'or long settlement, and lies under the 1300 foot Longstone Edge. Like most of the surrounding villages it once relied on lead mining and sheep farming although the latter is still prevalent along with large herds of mainly black and white cows. Today there are still working farms and a good variety of tradesmen.

The Main Street is lined with interesting buildings erected over the last 300-400 years and the focal point is the ancient village cross. The house behind was a pub known as the Miners Arms.

HAWTHORNE COTTAGE
GREAT LONGSTONE

HENRY EDWARDS 1995

LOOKING FROM THE SCHOOL GREAT LONGSTONE BRIAN EDWARDS 1998.

Hawthorne Cottage overlooks the green where markets were once held. In later years there were fairs here and these days carol singing around the tree.

Looking from the school over Main Street with the well dressing tableau by the tree. In the middle ground is Church Lady House a late medieval house; the date stone refers to an 18th century renovation. Just behind is the Shakerley building with a date stone of 1667 but much altered in recent years.

Thornbridge 'Manor' stands close to the old
railway line and the boundary between
Longstone and Ashford.

GATES TO GREAT LONGSTONE HALL   BRIAN EDWARDS 1995.   40.

DOWN STATION ROAD GREAT LONGSTONE   BRIAN EDWARDS 1996.

Looking down Station Road you can see
Longstone Hall built, unusually for the area,
in red brick with stone quoins and
surrounds. There was certainly an earlier
building on the site and part of its' stone
structure can still be seen. The Hall can also
be glimpsed through the old gateway on
Main Street.

When I produce finished drawings of
buildings I often make a series of sketches to
establish the viewpoint and proportions.
This is a preliminary drawing of the Tithe
Barn, shown in detail overleaf.

THE TITHE BARN GREAT LONGSTONE BRIAN EDWARDS

Referred to as the Tithe Barn, this early 19th
century building was partly burnt down
some years ago and substantially rebuilt. It
formed part of a group of farm buildings
around Longstone Hall.

THE CORNER GREAT LONGSTONE
BRIAN EDWARDS 1996

The view down Butts Road shows, right to
left, the stables, coach house and tithe barn.
All are now dwelling houses. In the centre is
an old trough and pump used as a water
supply well into the 20th century and in the
background is the Hall.

Church Lane Great Longstone 642. / Brian Edwards 1995

Church Lane Great Longstone 1993   Brian Edwards '98.

Sadly Church Lane, shown left, has been shorn of it's mature trees of recent years but the approach from Hassop is still overhung, framing the church quite nicely.

The church of St. Giles at Great Longstone was established in the 13th century although little remains from that era. There is much evidence of major rebuilding exercises in the fourteenth and fifteenth centuries and of course there was major work carried out in 1872. An excellent authoritative and informative booklet is available in the church.

ST GILES
GREAT LONGSTONE
BRIAN EDWARDS
1996 FOR MICK BRIGGS

616   THE BARN ON CHURCH LANE   GREAT LONGSTONE   BRIAN EDWARDS 1995.

MARCH 1990.
OLD TROUGHS AT
GREAT LONGSTONE
BRIAN EDWARDS

BRIAN EDWARDS   820   1   GT LONGSTONE CHURCH LANE FARM 1996

BRIAN EDWARDS 1998.

Dale Farm stands at the side of the leafy old trackway known as Chertpit Lane. An old cast iron pump stands as a reminder of harder times.

Church Lane Farm is very much part of Great Longstone Village and has a group of eighteenth century buildings ranged around the farmyard. The troughs replenished by a small stream are a source of enjoyment to villagers calling at the dairy for their milk. There is a separate old barn across the road (above left).

Thankfully a number of old stone field barns are still in use although some smaller ones have either decayed or been pulled down. Top: near Rowland and bottom: above Little Longstone.

PACKHORSE BRIDGE BAKEWELL BRIAN EDWARDS 1996 ©
for Bill + Bren.

Lumford packhorse bridge built in 1664 once connected Bakewell with Longstone but the boundary was moved much closer to the latter in the 19th century. On the far side can be seen the stables to Holme Hall. Close by is the old sheep wash fold.

DRIVING THE SHEEP GREAT LONGSTONE 1997 BRIANEDWARDS

Several times each year sheep are driven through the village filling the air with their loud bleating. I usually rush to the gateway hoping to catch a glimpse.

BRIAN EDWARDS '96
MOOR ROAD GT. LONGSTONE

There are a number of attractive outlying farms and houses in Great Longstone. Gild Low stands high above the village with views beyond Matlock.

Another approach to Great Longstone - this one descends from Longstone Edge hence it's name Moor Road. The fell runners toil up here on the tough ascent before clattering back down to the recreation ground in the annual race.

BRIAN EDWARDS 1998   MOOR ROAD GREAT LONGSTONE

FROM LONGSTONE EDGE
BRIAN EDWARDS 1997.

The panoramic views from Longstone Edge are quite spectacular over the Chatsworth Estate and the Wye Valley and north towards the gritstone country. We all marvel at the hard work that went into the building of so many dry stone walls.

In the foreground, above, the allotments fringe one approach to Great Longstone. Referred to as 'The Mires' the area was once the collecting point for the various watercourses running down the village. Lead miners are said to have separated away their ore nearby.

Looking back at 'The Mires' once known as Town End.

Great Longstone is fortunate in retaining many and varied mature trees. The limes enable the bees to produce a distinctive honey bottled and sold in the village shop.

GREAT LONGSTONE THROUGH TREES   BRIAN EDWARDS 1995

Above, Great Longstone through the trees sketched from one of the footpaths. Right and old cottage on Main Street with a date stone of 1772 and the initials of Martin and Ann Furniss who had much land scattered throughout the district. It is thought that in the 1840's it was a beer house referred to as Uncle Tom's Cabin.

BRIAN EDWARDS 1995.

The farm at the junction of Butts Road with Moor Road parted from it's original use some years ago and is now a dwelling house.

Set in secluded grounds, the Croft Country House Hotel was formerly a farm belonging to the Duke of Devonshire's estate. It was converted and extended to create a large private house in Victorian times.

LONGSTONE MOOR FARM
BRIAN EDWARDS 1995

Longstone Moor was described in 1764 as *very mountainous and rocky and utterly incapable of improvement and covered with heaps of rubbish where lead mines have been carried on.* The lead mines have gone but quarrying for fluorspar is still continued; only recently and application for a huge limestone quarrying operation was turned down. Longstone Moor Farm was once a gamekeepers lodge and was turned into a farm in 1944.

THE CROFT HOTEL GREAT LONGSTONE
BRIAN EDWARDS 2/97.

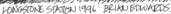

LONGSTONE STATION 1996 BRIAN EDWARDS.

Station Road leads off from the village green and was once known as Mill Lane supposedly because it led to the corn mill at Ashford. In the last century it became the main route to Longstone station and above I have drawn the hump back bridge over the line.

UP STATION ROAD GREAT LONGSTONE BRIAN EDWARDS 1996.

THE OLD STATION GREAT LONGSTONE AUTUMN 1996.
BRIAN EDWARDS MARCH 1997

The station at Great Longstone was opened in 1861 on the London to Manchester railway line. Closed in 1962, six years before the line was discontinued, the station, house and platforms are still visible from the Monsal trail. This walking and cycling track uses the old line and plans are underfoot to eventually reopen the line from Buxton to Matlock. We may yet see puffs of steam in the village.

Great Longstone is certainly not a single road
village and has a number of small lanes and
yards. This one, Spring Bank, runs from
Main Street to the recreation ground.

One of several in the village, Wardlow Yard
once housed a weavers workshop. At one
time the area had a flourishing trade started
by Flemish workers and a number of
stocking workshops were established.

MELLORS BUTCHERS SHOP
GREAT LONGSTONE   BRIAN EDWARDS 1996   641

Great Longstone is fortunate in having a
family run village store, post office and this
family butchers at which three generations
ply their trade.
Just opposite the butchers shop is this
unusual wooden house.

MAIN STREET
GREAT LONGSTONE   BRIAN EDWARDS 1996   A3

GT LONGSTONE CHURCH PATH.
BRIAN EDWARDS 1992.

PATH FROM THE CHURCH GREAT LONGSTONE 1996
BRIAN EDWARDS

At either end of this short path from Main Street to the church are wrought iron kissing gates in working order.

There are three school buildings, the upper
school of 1862 with it's modern extension
and then there is the above infants school of
1875, now used for the under fives, and
illustrated above.
The junior school is well attended and is
even planning a new classroom.

MANOR BARN   GREAT LONGSTONE   BRIAN EDWARDS 1996

On the left, with the chimneys, is the Manor House reputed to be the oldest dwelling in Great Longstone and dating from the early 17th century.

In the centre of the drawing is the former barn and cheese factory with the manager's cottage to the right. They stand back from Main Street just above the Crispin Inn.

THE OLD HARROW AND WHITE LION   BRIAN EDWARD 1996

The White Lion is the more recent of the pubs in Great Longstone, and earlier one of that name was converted into the vicarage during the last century !

Yet another pub 'The Harrow' was once located in the detached house below the present White Lion.

One of the village pumps once outside has recently been rediscovered and is due for installing near the renovated Village Hall.

CRISPIN INN GREAT LONGSTONE. 1994.
BRIAN EDWARDS.

At one time there were several pubs in Longstone and two remain. The Crispin, standing well back, was named after the patron saint of shoemaking which suggests a modest footwear industry sometime in the past.

The cottages to the left formed one side of Bullfinch Square named after Ralph Finch, manager of a local cotton mill. The dwelling on the right was once a slaughter house.

TRACK OFF BUTTS ROAD GREAT LONGSTONE

BRIAN EDWARDS 1996.

Right, one of the cart tracks leading from Butts Road into the fields.

Rowland

Rowland is a tiny hamlet which had ten farms in the 16th century until the village was acquired by Rowland Eyre of Hassop 'who decayed all the farms and tenements' supposedly to further his sheep farming ambitions. Here again the village relied on the lead mining industry and traces can still be seen in the vicinity.

This small farm remains much as it was a hundred years ago alongside the lane. What a peaceful place.

Rowland

I liked the contrast between the old
farmhouse and the arched corrugated
outbuilding. Longstone Edge forms the
backdrop to the little backwater of Rowland.

Hassop

Hassop is a tiny hamlet hardly deserving the powerful reputation it held for centuries. However it has some interesting buildings including the Hall, church and a 17th century manor house with a post box let into it's walls.

Hassop Hall was once the seat of the powerful Eyre family and is mainly seventeenth century with alterations and extensions in the period 1827/33. It is now a hotel and restaurant and has a series of interesting outbuildings and a main lodge. Another lodge on the Bakewell Road has finely carved stonework and stands behind well crafted and intricate wrought iron gates.

On the road from Bakewell stands this fine 17th century Manor House now divided into three separate dwellings. The three gables present a strong focal point on the village approach.

Rowdale Toll Bar cottage was positioned to control the cross roads coming from Bakewell via Lumford Packhorse Bridge and then on to Rowland and beyond. The remains of the other road from the Chatsworth direction can still be seen, on the field opposite the cottage, as a raised green trackway.

HASSOP 1998 BRIAN EDWARDS.

THE TOLL HOUSE HASSOP
BRIAN EDWARDS 1997

Down a winding lane from Hassop to
Baslow is the old catholic village school
complete with bell. It is now a house
having closed earlier this century.

Park Farm comprises a long range of
buildings including the half brick half stone
house.
The wooded grounds to Hassop Hall form
the backcloth.

Several of the old barns in Hassop have
been successfully converted into homes.
This 17th century building is known as the
Piggeries and the demolition of the lean-to
has exposed a fine row of stone arches.

FARM HASSOP BRIAN EDWARDS 1997.

BARN AT HASSOP BRIAN EDWARDS 1996.

HASSOP DERBYSHIRE
BRIAN EDWARDS 1991

HASSOP CHURCH 1991
BRIAN EDWARDS

All Saints Church in Hassop is an Etruscan
influenced building with small colonnade -
quite imposing for such a small hamlet. It
was built by the Catholic Eyre family in
1816/18 and overshadows the Dower House.

THE EYRE ARMS AT HASSOP   BRIAN EDWARDS 1996 ©

The Eyre Arms stands proudly at the roadside in Hassop and in autumn is smothered in crimson red ivy. Inside is the Coat of Arms of the Eyre family with a single leg clad in armour - pop in and read about the legend behind the leg. A farm of 1640 was converted into the pub thirty years later.

Built in 1863-7 by Edward Walters and of a typical design for the Duke of Devonshire at nearby Chatsworth, Hassop Station closed in 1942. Nowadays it houses a country bookstore whilst across the trackway is the refurbished station house.

COUNTRY BOOKSTORE
HASSOP STATION FEB.1987 BRIAN EDWARDS

Index

Please note that because the villages are named so
numerously in the text, they are not included in the index.

Bibliography

The Peak District National Park, it's architecture - John Tarn
The Derbyshire Country House - Maxwell Craven & Michael Stanley
The Derbyshire Village Book - Derbyshire Federation of Women's Institures
Recollections of Bakewell - Trevor Brighton & Frank Saunders
A Gazetteer of the White Peak - Les Robson
For a more detailed history of Great Longstone see The Village Trail published by the Longstone Local History Group. Available in local shops.